Real Read to Write

Writing for the Real World

Written by
Judith S. Gould
& Mary F. Burke

Illustrated by Shelly S. Rasche

Teaching & Learning Company
1204 Buchanan St., P.O. Box 10
Carthage, IL 62321-0010

Cover design by Sara King

Cover illustrations by Shelly S. Rasche

Copyright © 2007, Teaching & Learning Company

ISBN 13: 978-1-57310-486-9

ISBN 10: 1-57310-486-3

Printing No. 987654321

Teaching & Learning Company
1204 Buchanan St., P.O. Box 10
Carthage, IL 62321-0010

Table of Contents

Writing for Your Neighborhood and Beyond

Card Number

1. Writing a Letter
2. Writing to Newspapers and Magazines
3. Writing to Assisted-Living Residences
4. Writing to Authors
5. Writing to Elected Officials
6. Writing to Athletes
7. Writing to Musicians
8. Writing to Celebrities
9. Writing to Pen Pals
10. Writing to Deployed Armed Forces
11. Writing to Retail Companies
12. Writing to Get Free Stuff
13. Writing a Postcard
14. Writing a Greeting Card
15. Writing to Get Published

Writing for Your School

Card Number

16. Writing a Special Announcement
17. Writing a Visitor's Guide to the School
18. Writing a Script for a Television Production
19. Writing a Program for a Performance or Assembly
20. Writing a Handbook for Substitutes
21. Writing an Invitation
22. Writing to Local Business Partners
23. Writing an Advertisement
24. Writing a Letter to the Incoming Class
25. Writing an Interview with a Teacher

Writing for Yourself, Your Family and Your Friends

Card Number

26. Writing an "All by Myself" Poem
27. Writing a Biographical Poem
28. Writing an Acrostic Phrase Poem
29. Writing an Onomatopoeia Poem
30. Writing a "You Make Me So Mad" Poem
31. Writing an "Odd Squad" Poem
32. Writing a "Happy Place" Poem
33. Writing a 5 Ws Poem
34. Writing a Recipe Poem
35. Writing an Alliteration Poem
36. Writing a "Looking Back" Poem
37. Writing a "Friends Forever" Poem
38. Writing a Portrait Poem
39. Writing a Favorites Poem
40. Writing an "I Wish" Poem
41. Writing a "That's Mine" Poem
42. Writing an "Oh No" Poem
43. Writing to Yourself
44. Writing in a Journal

Introduction

It is rare indeed to meet a teacher who has complete control over the writing curriculum. We live in a time when the choices concerning our writing instruction are made for us by school districts and state mandates. Students write to meet standards established by strangers. Unless students have had the opportunity to write for a real reason—a personal reason unique to their lives—they can't begin to understand the rationale for revision or proofing, for choosing the right word or for making sure a sentence reads smoothly and is punctuated perfectly. We are asking students to play make-believe with our instruction unless it's connected to their real world. That connection is essential for our students if writing is to take on any value in their lives.

Fortunately, amid all these requirements for "fake writing" (as our friend Barry Lane likes to describe it), we know there are teachers who throw caution to the wind. They dare to challenge and inspire their students to write for authentic reasons—real reasons students define for themselves.

We offer these ideas to encourage the notion of real writing—writing that comes from a need to share the creative and expressive self in each of us.

Sincerely,

Judith Mary

Judith S. Gould & Mary F. Burke

Writing a Letter

Maybe it's not as fast as e-mail or a text message, but a letter is a gift that comes in an envelope. A letter is a compliment. It means that the sender was thinking of you and only you for the time it took to write it. No wonder people save their letters. Who would throw away a compliment?

When you write a letter, remember to:

- Sound like yourself.
- Tell the person why you are writing.
- Use specific details.
- Be polite.
- Express yourself clearly.

Writing to Newspapers and Magazines

Is something going on in the news that has you thinking? Is there a current event in your school or in your town that makes you want to shout? You can shout and maybe even be published! Writing a letter to the editor of a newspaper or magazine lets the publishers know that real people are reading and thinking about their writing.

Writing Tips

- Have a formal manner; this is not a friendly letter.
- State your position clearly and support it with your reasons.
- Never, ever insult an editor.
- Keep it short—not longer than one page.
- Make sure your letter is proofread properly before you send it.

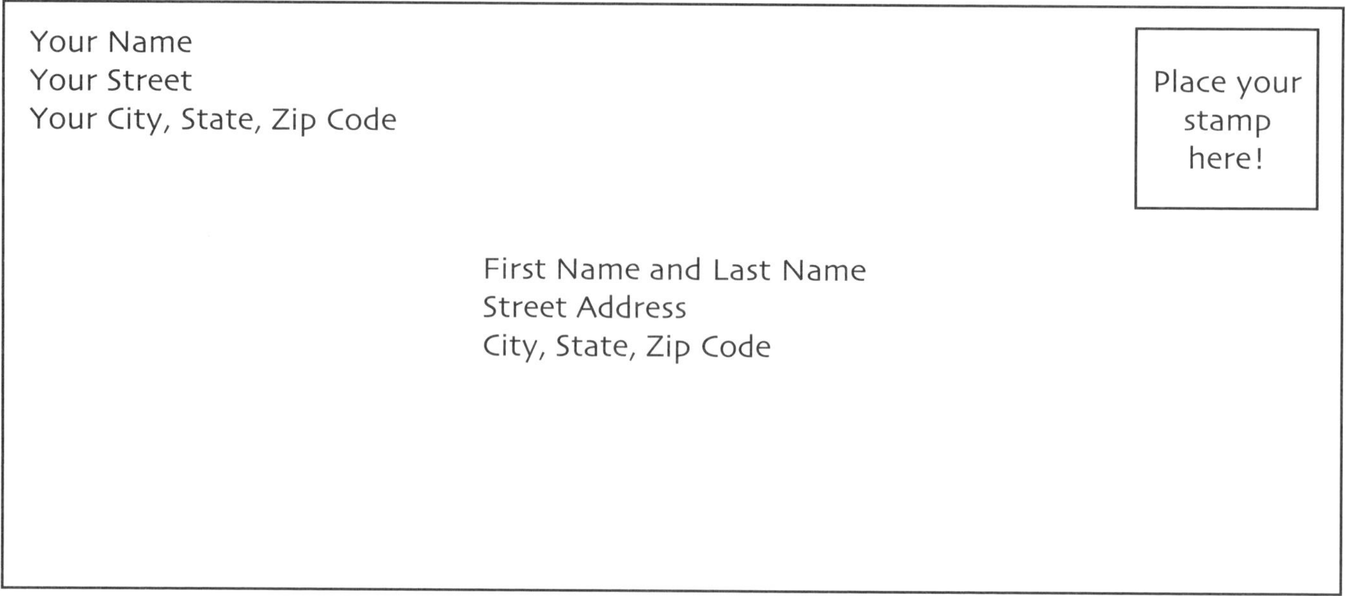

Shorter is better when it comes to a letter to the editor! Before you write, it is a good idea to know exactly what you want to say, and then stick to it. One main idea will be more than enough for your letter. Planning is the best way to write short and powerful letters.

Try a Four Square for a planning tool.

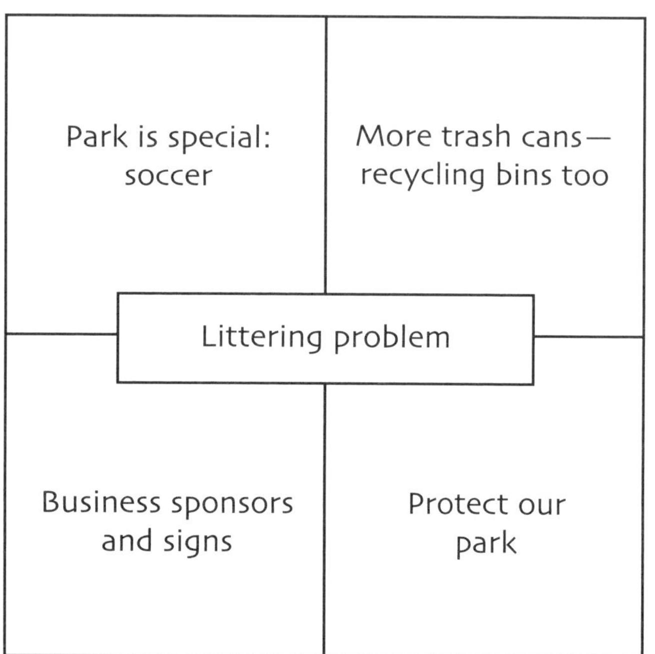

November 28, 2006

To the Editor of the Burkeville Times:

   As a student at Burkeville Elementary, I am very concerned about the littering problem in Martin Park. This park is a very special place to me and my friends. We have played soccer there since I was little. I think that more trash cans would help people to keep the park clean. People would even recycle if bins were there for our cans and bottles. Maybe there are some businesses in town who can donate these trash cans. Then we could put a sign on the can, and everyone would want to shop at those stores. I definitely believe we need to do everything we can to protect our park.

                              Sincerely,

                              Your Name

Writing to Assisted-Living Residences

Write a letter to someone to give them a smile. This letter will go to someone who is living in a home apart from their family, so your friendly words will warm someone's heart. Ask a parent or a teacher for the address of an assisted-living residence near you.

Writing Tips

- Sound like yourself.
- Don't ask personal questions.
- Tell about yourself (but don't tell anything your family wouldn't want you to share).
- Include something special like a drawing, poem or joke.
- Write neatly! Spell well.

Writing to Authors

We love their books and we want to know more about them and how they do their writing. Many authors will respond to kids' writing. (A great book to read is Beverly Cleary's *Dear Mr. Henshaw*) Find an author's address on the title page in care of the publisher. Check publisher's Web sites. They often have links. Or ask a teacher or parent to help you find the address.

Writing Tips

- Send a self-addressed, stamped envelope if you want a reply.
- Any questions you ask should be relevant to the author's writing.
- Keep your letter to one page.
- The tone should be friendly and polite.

This type of writing is called a friendly letter. Use this format for your letter.

Some salutations:
Dear __________
To __________
My friend __________

Date

Salutation,

Body of your letter. This is where your sentences and paragraphs go. Remember to indent each paragraph!

Closing,
Your Name

Some closings:

Your friend,
Sincerely,
Truly,
Fondly,

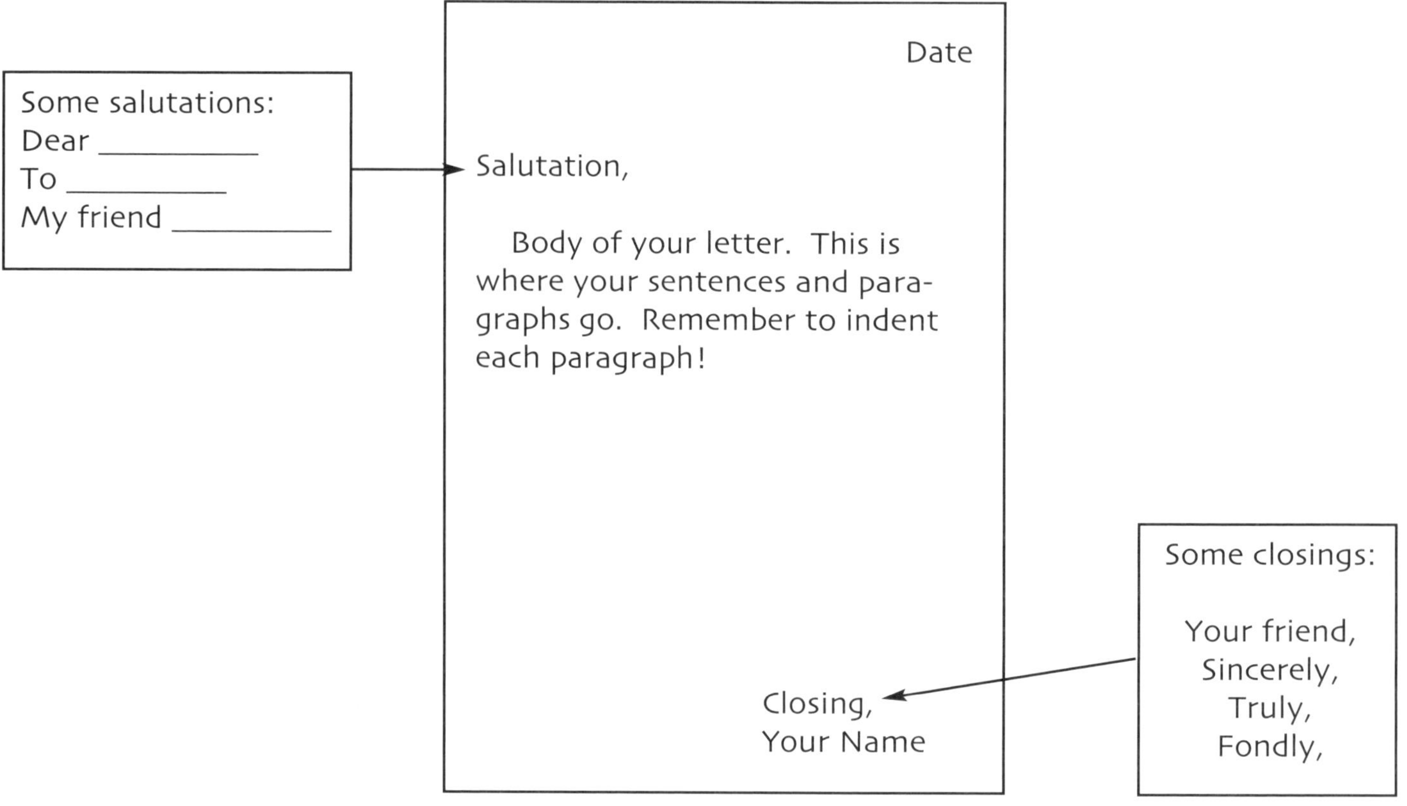

Here's a sample to give you some ideas.

March 25, 2007

Mr. Andrew Clements
c/o Best Book Publishers
123 TLC Street
New York, NY 11111

Dear Mr. Clements:

I am a fifth-grade student who attends Paterson Elementary School. I just finished reading your book *The Last Holiday Concert.* I chose to read this book because music is one of my favorite classes.

I am writing this letter to thank you for such a wonderful book. I liked the way the characters handled the problems they faced. It seemed to me that the music teacher learned a lot from his experience.

Was music a favorite subject for you too? Is that why you wrote this?

Please keep writing these wonderful stories. I will read everything you write.

Sincerely,
Your Name

First introduce yourself and tell why you're writing.

Include a compliment or a comment for the author. Be specific.

Ask a question or two.

End with a friendly good-bye.

Writing to Elected Officials

Write to those who can make change happen. Many kids can have strong feelings about the environment, social programs, crime and, of course, education. Our words and our votes make this democracy great. Let the elected officials know what kids are thinking and feeling.

Writing Tips

- Include your address.
- Any questions you ask should be relevant to the issues contained in your letter.
- Be polite and respectful.
- Use appropriate titles.
- Focus on one issue per letter.
- Keep your letter to one page, if possible.

Writing to Athletes

You love to watch them play, now let them hear what you have to say! Fan letters are a great way to show your appreciation. Who knows, you may even get a reply! Write to your favorite athlete in care of their team or league.

Writing Tips

- Tell why you are writing.
- Do not ask for free merchandise or special favors.
- Ask questions about their professional career—nothing too personal!
- Be polite and respectful.
- Keep your letter to one page, if possible.
- Include a self-addressed, stamped envelope if you would like a reply.

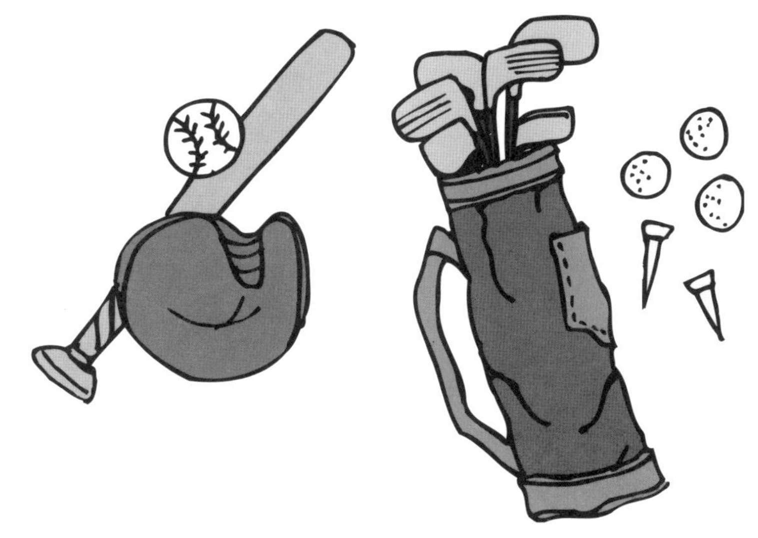

Here are some addresses for the elected officials in Washington, D.C.

The general address for the U.S. Senate is:
The Honorable _______________
U.S. Senate
Washington, D.C. 20510

President _______________
The White House
1600 Pennsylvania Avenue, NW
Washington, D.C. 20500

The general address for the
U.S. House of Representatives is:
The Honorable _______________
U.S. House of Representatives
Washington, D.C. 20515

Vice President _______________
The White House
1600 Pennsylvania Avenue, NW
Washington, D.C. 20500

Ask an adult to help you find addresses for local officials.

The self-addressed, stamped envelope is one way to convince a reader that you really would like a reply to their letter. To do this, you include an empty envelope inside your letter. Be sure to write your name and address on the front of the empty envelope, and put a stamp on it too!

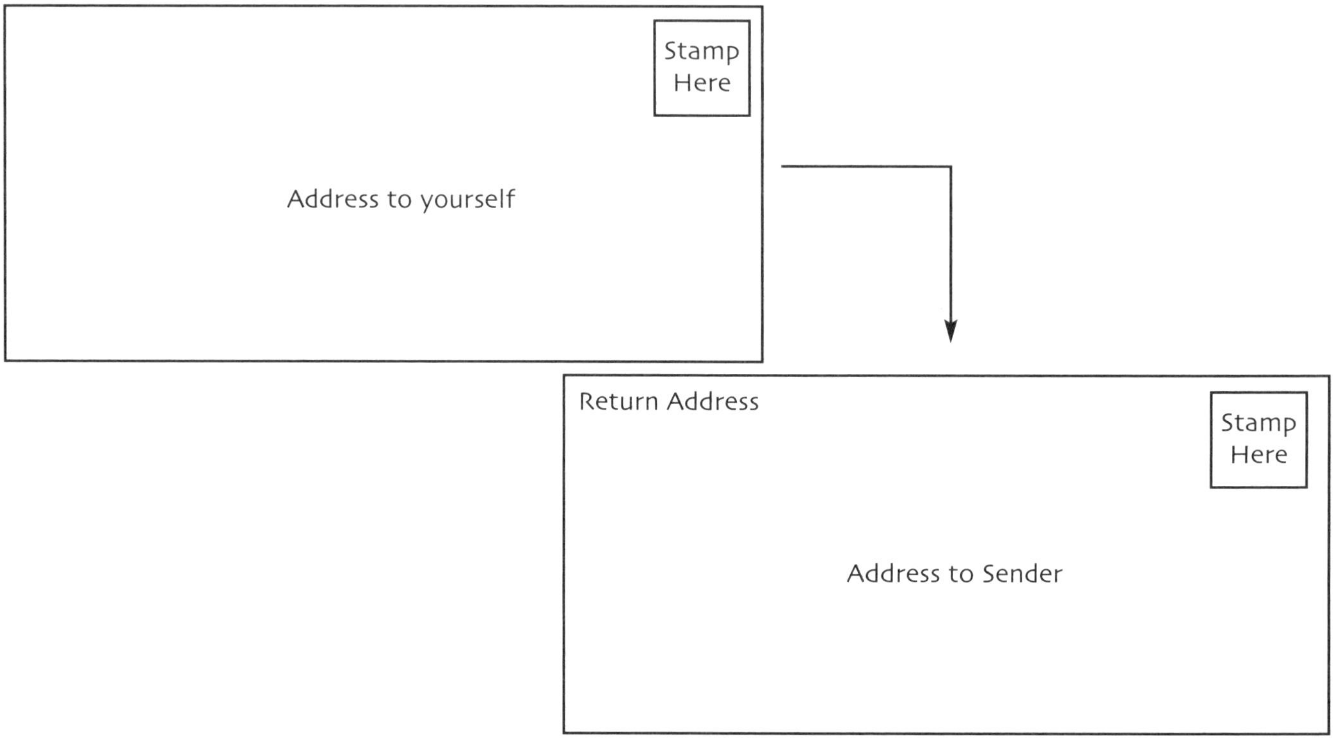

Stamp Here

Address to yourself

Return Address

Stamp Here

Address to Sender

Writing to Musicians

Most entertainers love to hear from their audiences. This is a great way to cheer for the band, even if you are not at the concert. Let the musicians know how and why you listen to their music. Tell about your favorite parts.

Writing Tips

- Be yourself.
- Tell why you are writing.
- Do not ask for free merchandise or special favors.
- Any questions should be relevant to the music or the musician's career.
- Be polite and respectful.
- Keep your letter to one page.

Writing to Celebrities

They're famous, they're fabulous and they're people too! Top-rated celebrities receive countless letters, so don't bank on response. But that makes the rare response from these busy people even more special.

Writing Tips

- Any questions should be relevant to the entertainer's career.
- Be polite and respectful.
- Keep your letter to one page.
- A 9" x 11" pre-paid envelope might come back with an autographed picture.

Write to a recording artist in care of their label. For example, imagine that you want to write to your favorite band, The Screaming Geeks, who have a CD on the Wild Thing label. This is how to address the envelope.

<table>
<tr><td>

Your Name
Your Street
Your City, State, Zip Code

</td><td>

Place your
stamp
here!

</td></tr>
<tr><td colspan="2">

The Screaming Geeks
C/O Wild Thing Recordings
123 Musical Way
Harmony, USA 12345

</td></tr>
</table>

Keeping up a list of addresses for who's hot and who's not would be a full-time job. Fortunately, technology can help us find addresses. Many celebrities have fan clubs you can access on the Internet. Ask an adult to help you search for an address. Remember, you don't need to join the fan club to send a letter.

You might also check your local library for one of these titles. They list hundreds of celebrities' mailing addresses.

The Celebrity Black Book: Over 40,000 Celebrity Addresses
    by Jordan McAuley (Editor), Mega Niche Media, 2004.

The Celebrity Address Directory & Autograph Collector's Guide
    by Lee A. Ellis, Americana Group Publishing, 2002.

Free Autographs by Mail: 4,000+ Verified Celebrity Addresses
    by Cynthia Mattison, Writer's Club Press, 2000.

Alan Gottlieb's Celebrity Address Book
    by Alan Gottlieb, Merrill Press, 2000.

Writing to Pen Pals

Sure, you could have an electronic pen pal. But isn't it more mysterious to imagine the journey of your little envelope? It is in your hands right now, but in a few days that very same envelope will be in a place far, far away. Make a friend through the mail who just might become a friend for life.

Writing Tips

- Write about yourself, then ask a few questions about your pen pal.
- Avoid controversial topics.
- Keep it friendly.
- Use your real voice for communication. You want to let your pen pal know who you really are.
- Be careful not to reveal too much personal information. Remember: A pen pal starts off as a stranger.

Writing to Deployed Armed Forces

A personal letter from back home can be a great gift for someone who is giving so much for the country. Writing and keeping up-to-date with a soldier can put a smile on the face of someone far away from home.

Writing Tips

- Tell about yourself, your school and your community.
- Neatness counts.
- Don't ask specific questions about a soldier's mission—they may not be allowed to discuss it.
- Do ask questions about the soldier's daily routine and what it's like to serve in the armed forces.

Before starting, it's a good idea to plan. Use this list as a way to collect information about yourself that you would like to share with your pen pal.

1. Your name.
2. Age and birthday
3. Brothers/Sisters/Family members at home
4. Pets you have or wish you could have
5. Hobbies
6. Favorite foods
7. Foods you would never, ever eat (and why)
8. Your idea of a fantastic day
9. Your idea of a bummer of a day
10. What your school is like

Not sure what to write? Here's an example.

Put your return address inside the letter. These envelopes have to travel many miles, and the outside may be smeared or damaged.

c/o Johnson Elementary School
715 Route 17
Anyplace, USA Zip Code

October 22, 2006

Dear Soldier,

   I am a fourth-grade student at Johnson Elementary School in Anyplace. I love living in the U.S.A., especially in my town where everyone is friendly. I have played soccer for 5 years, and one day I will be a pro. Both my parents work in the assembly plant here, and most families in town do too. — 1. Tell about yourself and your town.

   I wanted to write to you to thank you for doing what you are doing. You help to keep us safe, and I hope you get back home safely, too. — 2. Tell why you are writing.

   Do you miss your family? Do you have any kids? Any in fourth grade? It must be hard work that you do every day. I would love it if you have time to write me back. — 3. Ask a couple of questions.

        Sincerely,
        Your Name

Writing to Retail Companies

Think about the things you buy or your family buys for you. Are you satisfied with the performance, appearance or price of these products? What would you like to change? What would you like to compliment? Writing to retail companies is an opportunity to voice your feelings about all sorts of products.

Positive letters to a company may actually result in a personal reply, coupons for other products or maybe even some free stuff! You won't know until you try it, so go ahead. Make your consumer voice be heard!

Writing Tips

- This business letter should have a formal tone.
- Even with a complaint, be respectful. Nobody wants to read a letter full of angry accusations, and it will not be taken as serious correspondence.
- Be brief and to the point.
- If this is a complaint or concern, state what you feel would be fair compensation.
- If you are looking for compensation, include copies of UPC codes or receipts.

Writing to Get Free Stuff

What's better than buying new stuff? Getting FREE stuff! And yes, there are ways you can write to get free stuff! There are all sorts of companies that will send you samples of their products if you write to them. So, what are you waiting for? These books provide tips and addresses:

Free Stuff for Kids, by the Free Stuff Editors, Meadowbrook Publishers, 2005.
Free Stuff & Good Deals for Your Kids, by Linda Bowman, Santa Monica Press, 2002.
Free Stuff for Everyone! by Barbara Bectrer, Prime Publishers, Inc., 2001.

Writing Tips

- These are business letters, so they should have a formal tone.
- Look for the fine print. You may have to pay some shipping and handling.
- Free offers expire. Read each offer carefully.

Here is a sample letter. (Note the business letter form)

1414 Knights Trail
Queens, NY 10036

January 17, 2007

US Chess Federation
3054 Route 9W
New Windsor, NY 12553

Dear Sirs:

   I am just learning how to play chess, and I would very much like the official rules so I can memorize them. In the *Free Stuff* book, it also said that you would send me the booklet *10 Tips to Winning Chess* upon request. This is my official request for that booklet. Thank you very much.

Sincerely,
Jo Chesslover

Here is a sample letter.

Dear Gaming Gamers Company,

   Recently I was at a discount store looking for your game, Jeepers. I wanted to bring it to Game Day at school, but my little brother lost a bunch of the pieces to the one we had at home. I was really surprised when the game was listed as $12.99. There was this identical game right next to it, same sized pieces, same amount of pieces, the only difference was that the word *Jeepers* was not printed on each piece of the game. That identical game was priced at $3.49.

   Of course, since I was buying this with my own money, I bought the lower priced game and saved over $8.50. You should really consider lowering the price of Jeepers, because if a kid like me can figure this out, I'm sure a lot of grown-ups can too.

Sincerely,
Your Name

Writing a Postcard

Maybe you know the postcard as a little picture you receive from friends and family on vacation. But postcards can be fun to write every day too! You can make a postcard out of a photograph, or even on a plain index card. Then you can become the writer *and* the illustrator. Here's a nice bonus: postcards are less expensive to mail than letters!

Writing Tips

- Write the address clearly.
- Remember to leave a spot for the stamp.
- This is a short message. Use strong words to get the job done.
- Because a postcard doesn't go into an envelope, anyone can read it. Don't write anything too personal.

Writing a Greeting Card

Why pay as much as $5.00 for a card when you can make one yourself? All it takes is a little creativity and a few craft supplies. You don't even need to wait for a holiday to send a card. An ordinary day can become special when you give a card to someone just to let them know you were thinking of them.

Writing Tips

- Look at some old greeting cards for ideas.
- You may choose to rhyme your message or not.
- This is usually a short piece of writing, so choose your words carefully. Powerful words get the job done. For example, instead of writing "I hope you have a nice birthday," write "Wishing you a bodacious birthday blast!"

It's easy (and fun) to make a postcard out of an index card. Use the kind that has lines on one side. The blank side is yours to illustrate. The other side is where your writing goes. Use this as a guide for the space on your writing side.

Your message goes here.

Stamp Here

Person's Name

Street Address

City, State, Zip

Country

Use some cardstock or construction paper to make your greeting card sturdy. The front should have some art or illustration. You don't have to draw it yourself! Photographs, pictures or collages from magazines, or computer clip art can all jazz up a greeting card. You could even get fancy and glue on some dried flowers to decorate the front!

Front

A short greeting and some artwork.

Inside

Write a short message here.

Don't forget to sign your name!

Writing to Get Published

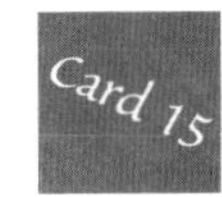

Writing is a real job. Some people choose to earn a living by writing (or maybe fate chooses them). This isn't an easy job. It means sharing your writing in a very public way. It means the possibility of strangers rejecting your writing. To be a writer, you need to be tough!

Writing is kind of like running a race against yourself. You try to make every word the best it can be. You try to make this piece of writing better than the one before it. Getting writing published is like winning the race.

Writing Tips

- Check out some of your favorite magazines to see if they accept submissions and to find the address for mailing them in.
- See if they have rules about the length and format of writing that is sent in.
- Neatness is really important!

Writing a Special Announcement

Writing for school? You're probably saying, "I already write tons of stuff for school—reports, stories, essays, all sorts of responses!!!"

We're talking about other kinds of writing that help a school. Every school is a busy place with lots of information that needs to go home. Why shouldn't you have a try at writing some of these notices that go home? School holiday coming up? Early release day approaching? Field trip on the way? PTA program being scheduled? This is all informational writing with a built-in audience for a REAL purpose.

Writing Tips

- Make sure you have all the facts right.
- Know your audience. Are you writing for students? Families? Teachers?
- Know your purpose for writing. What important information do you need to communicate.
- Neatness, spelling and grammar are important!

Here are the addresses of some popular publications that accept student writing:

Stone Soup
Submissions Department
P.O. Box 83
Santa Cruz, CA 95063

Highlights for Children
Business Office
1800 Watermark Drive
P.O. Box 269
Columbus, OH 43216

Check your school or local library for these two books. The offer great tips on getting your writing published.

The Young Writer's Guide to Getting Published
by Kathy Henderson, Writer's Digest Books, 2001.

Teen's Guide to Getting Published
by Danielle Dunn and Jessica Dunn, Prufrock Press, 1996.

Here is an example.

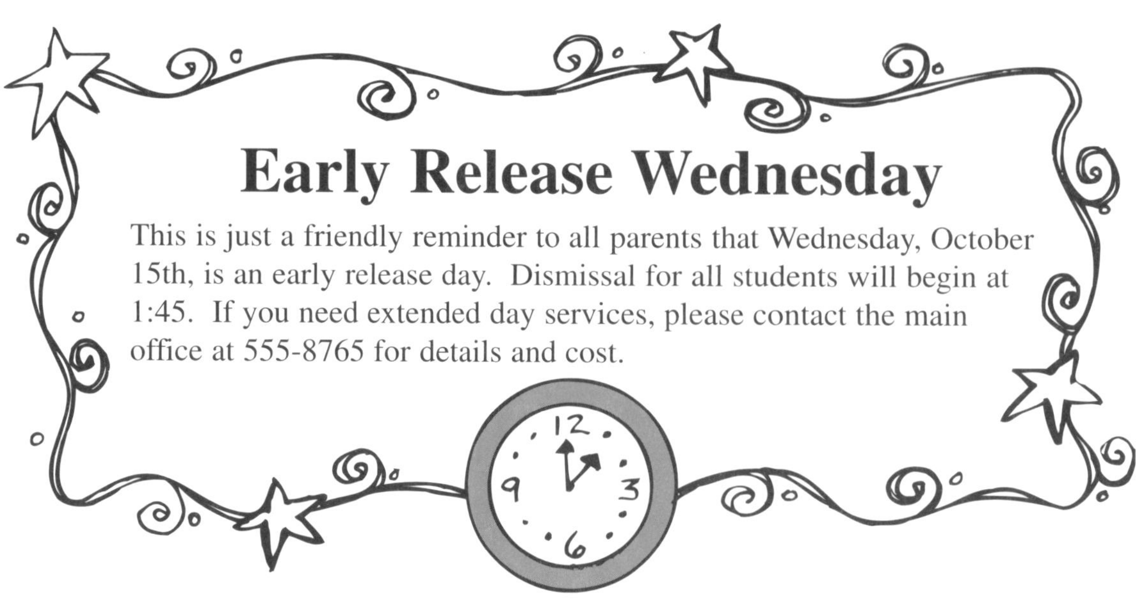

Writing a Visitor's Guide to the School

Who knows your school better than you? Think about how many people come through the doors of a school's front office: parents, substitute teachers, administrators, maintenance folks, salespeople, just to name a few. Sometimes these folks have to wait a bit before they can get to their business. Why not give them something interesting to read? A guide to your school, perhaps?

This is a big job so you may want to get some like-minded friends to help you with this. Look at guides from other schools to help you get started. Separate the job into different areas to cover. The guide can include a variety of facts and information. A page about the cafeteria, for instance, may introduce the kitchen staff, state the rules of the cafeteria and include a survey of favorite lunch menus. Add pictures and maps of the locations you write about, and add your own special voices to this project.

Writing Tips

- Individual pages can be laminated or placed in page protectors for a longer life.
- Put your best foot forward! This is not a place to be careless in spelling, handwriting or proofreading in general. People are going to read this!

Writing a Script for a Television Production

If you have a television production studio in your school, you may be interested in writing for television. This can include everything from informational to entertainment so many kinds of writing styles and writing voices are needed.

It might be helpful to watch different kinds of television programs for kids to get familiar with the writing styles aimed at young people. You may want to get in touch with the teacher who is in charge of television production at your school for more information. That person would have the final word on what is needed for their daily production.

Writing Tips

- Start with a catchy lead and make it short and sweet.
- Use literary devices (alliteration, exaggeration, etc).
- Know your English mechanics (spelling, grammar, punctuation).
- Check your facts.

Building Overview

The first floor of our school is where grade K-2 classes can be found. Also on this level is the main office, cafeteria, media center and guidance office. Classrooms for 3rd-5th grades can be found upstairs on the second floor. The second floor also houses the science lab, computer lab, Reading Recovery room, the music room and the art room.

The Main Office

Two wonderful secretaries run the main office. They are Mrs. Welby and Mrs. Crown. They answer phones, take messages, accept deliveries, loan out lunch money, put ice and bandages on cuts and bruises and help with car riders and bus riders during dismissal time. They know everything about everything and can answer all your questions.

Here is a sample script.

Anchor 1: Good morning and welcome to WFLE news.

Anchor 2: Your only source for news and information for Frederick Lincoln Elementary.

Anchor 1: Our top story today is that it's Career Day here at Lincoln Elementary. Speakers will be visiting every classroom and sharing info about what they do. We have doctors and lawyers coming, but we also have members of Life Flight and the SWAT team visiting too.

Anchor 2: Patrols will be acting as tour guides to our guests. Career Day speakers will begin at 9:00 a.m. and end at 10:30 a.m. We know everyone will enjoy listening to these interesting and unique speakers.

Writing a Program for a Performance or Assembly

The actors have practiced their parts. The musicians have learned the words to their songs or the notes for their instruments. If you happen to be one of the people involved in a performance, who better than you to prepare the written program for the audience?

In the program guide you will need to list the order of scenes, songs or speakers. Also required are things like dates, times and other important information, like names of performers and behind-the-scenes crew. Cover art on a program adds a nice touch, and a balanced layout of the written information will make the program more attractive and pleasant to read.

Writing Tips

- Proofreading is vital! Who hasn't heard of the nightmare of having a name misspelled or left out of a program? Remember, these programs are keepsakes for all involved.
- Be open to different kinds of ideas for the design and layout of the program. The best results of any project come from working together with enthusiasm.

Writing a Handbook for Substitutes

Why not make a substitute's day a little easier? Create a Substitute Teacher Guide. Not only will it make you a hero in your teacher's eyes (which might translate into less homework or more lenient deadlines for all sorts of projects), but it's a nice thing to do for those subs who brave a new class day after treacherous day.

Subs don't often have lots of preparation time for their classes so your class guide needs to be brief and full of information. Include things like the daily schedule, resources, locations where supplies are kept and what the procedure is for dismissal.

Writing Tips

- Make the guide on 5" x 7" index cards for easy readability.
- Include fun facts about you and your classmates.
- Write down your favorite recess activities or indoor games.

Here is part of a sample program.

Here is a sample of a page from a handbook for substitute teachers.

Dismissal Routine:

- Starts at 2:30.
- Each group takes turns going to their cubbies for their backpacks and packing up.
- Group leaders check agendas of their group members.
- Patrols are dismissed at 2:40.
- Students can read, write or draw, but they must stay quiet.
- Bus dismissal is on the TV on channel 4 starting at 2:45.
- Walkers and car riders are dismissed at 2:50 from the intercom.
- Extended Day students are dismissed at 3:10.

Writing an Invitation

The school year is full of all sorts of fun activities that involve families. There's Open House, Family Fun Day, Young Authors' Tea, Career Day—the list goes on! Why don't you get in on the planning and write up the invitations for those events at your school?

Writing Tips

- Be sure the information you include is accurate (time, date, place).
- Personalize the invitations with artwork and names.
- Write with energy and personality. Make sure the invitee knows this special invitation was written by you.

Writing to Local Business Partners

Does your teacher have a "wish list" of supplies posted? Is your class getting to the time of the year when some supplies are running low? Does your class need some things like tissues, anti-bacterial soap, or cotton balls for a special project? Write to a local business and ask if they would partner with your school to donate to your classroom. You never know what they will say until you ask!

Writing Tips

- Tell them specifically what you need and why.
- This is a business letter. Keep the tone friendly but formal.
- Show off the great education they are supporting. Look at how well we write (and revise and proofread). Make these super neat.
- Sending thank-you letters to these businesses isn't only friendly, they may need these as receipts for tax purposes.

Here is a sample invitation.

Open House

When: August 21st, 6:30 p.m.
Where: Room 201
Why: Get to know my teacher and how we do things in our classroom.

Do you wonder what I do all day long in school? How I use my agenda? What does my desk look like? Why my schedule is like it is? How the teacher formulates my grades? All these questions and more will be answered at Open House. Come and meet my teachers and say nice things about me! Meet other parents and get to know my world!

Take a look at this sample letter: Notice the business letter form.

Tell who you are and the class you are in. Share information about what you are learning.

Explain how their donation can help your learning.

Make your request specific.

Thank them for their time.

Jackson Elementary
219 Starry Street
Your Town, USA

December 1, 2006

People's Supermarket
317 Maple Road
Your Town, USA

Dear Store Manager,

I am a fifth-grade student in Mrs. Rosen's class. We are learning about molecules and other important things in Science class.

Mrs. Rosen says that we could do this exciting experiment where we turn cream into butter and then eat it. To do this we need to have a lot of cream so that every student can participate. My family shops at People's and most of the kids in my class do too. That's why I'm writing to ask if your store can donate six pints of cream so we can do this experiment. Mrs. Rosen wants to do the experiment on December 10th.

Thank you for taking the time to read this.

Sincerely,
Your Name

Writing an Advertisement

Special events happen all the time in schools. Plays, assemblies, spelling bees and concerts are just a few. Make sure that everyone knows about these coming events by writing and posting an advertisement.

Writing Tips

- Think about eye-catching slogans.
- Artwork is helpful in an advertisement.
- Make sure your writing is neat, clear and large enough to be read.
- Include specifics such as time and date.

Writing a Letter
to the Incoming Class

This school year you have learned a lot about many subjects. You're probably a better reader, mathematician, scientist and writer. You have also learned a lot about two other subjects: your grade and your teacher. As an expert in these areas, you can help a student new to the grade to be prepared. Write a letter to the student who will sit in your chair next year.

Writing Tips

- Include suggestions for getting along with your teacher.
- Tell a particular story that shows your teacher's personality.
- Preview some of the special projects or activities of the year.
- Share the likes and dislikes of your teacher.
- Give advice on how to have a great year.

Catchy slogans can help your advertisement really stand out.
Here are some examples of slogans for an advertisement for a school spelling bee.

Buzz on Over to the School's Spelling Bee	Using a play on words. Get it. It's not that kind of bee!
Don't BEE a Fool. Come to the Spelling Bee.	It's the play on words again!
Sit a Spell and See Some Super Spellers	Use many words starting with the same letter. This is called alliteration.
The Spelling Bee: A Must-See	Rhyming slogans are easy to remember.
To Bee or Not to Bee?	Imitate a famous saying.

Here is a sample letter.

Suggestions for Success ⟶

A Story ⟶

Projects ⟶

Advice ⟶

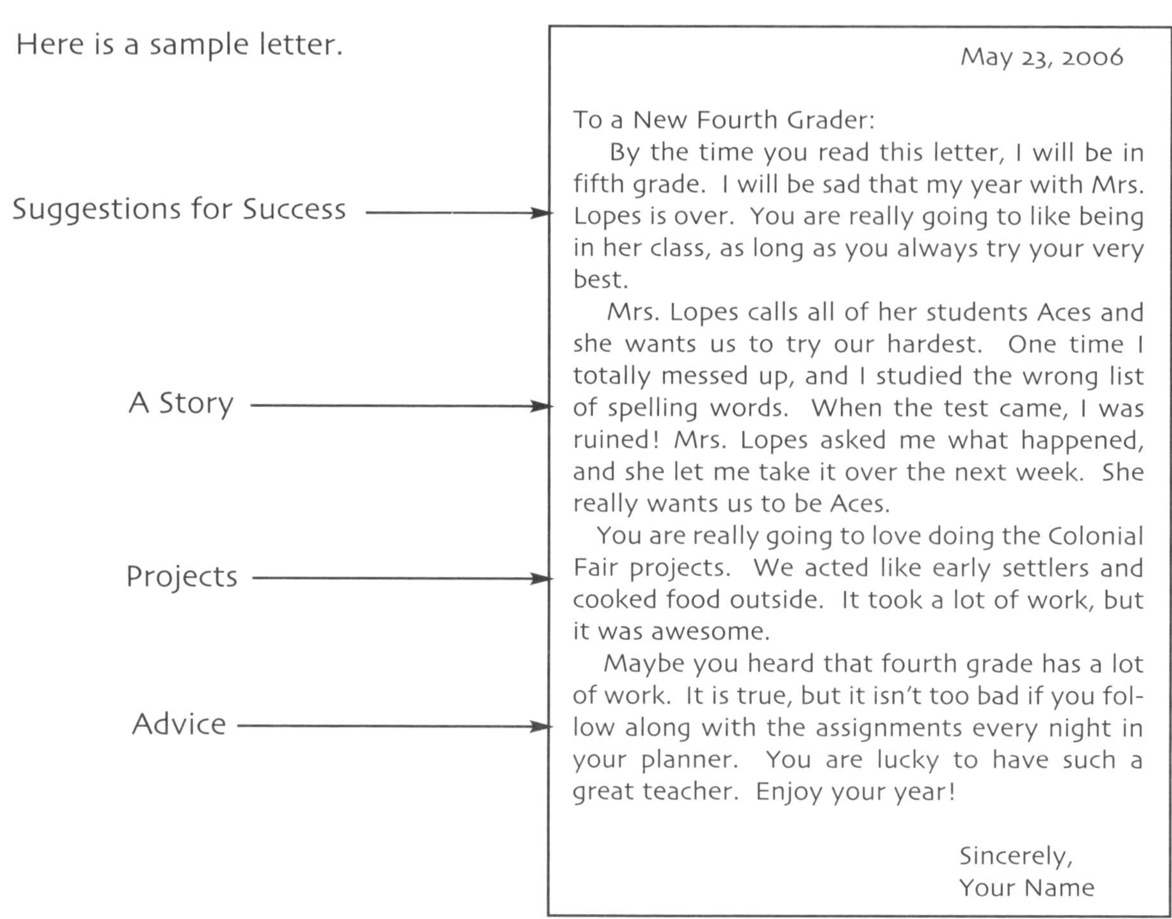

Writing an Interview with a Teacher

How much do you *really* know about the teachers at your school? Are there any things you would like to find out? Why not arrange an interview and find out more about the people who help you learn.

Writing Tips

- Set up an appointment to interview and be on time.
- Be prepared with a list of interesting questions to ask.
- Listen carefully to the answers. These answers might give you an idea for more questions to ask.
- Consider using a tape recorder to record the interview, but only with the person's permission.
- Share your interviews with others. Display them in the hallway, or make a book for the school library.

Writing an "All by Myself" Poem

There are times when we all find ourselves with no one around. Sometimes it can be lonely and other times it's a little peaceful. How do you feel when you are alone? Writing is a great way to put those feelings down. It's an easy thing to do when you're all by yourself.

Here's how to write this five-line poem:

1. When I am alone, I'm not by myself.
2. I have my ___________________ (one or more things you use) to keep me company.
3. Together we ___________________ (something you do together).
4. All by myself ___________________ (where you are).
5. End with a statement about how you feel during your alone time.

<u>Interview of Mr. Davis, Music Teacher</u>
Tuesday 11:15

1. Why did you decide to become a music teacher?

2. When did you first start being a musician?

3. What are some of your favorite instruments to play?

4. How do you choose the songs for the concerts?

Leave space to write answers.

Try not to ask yes/no questions. You want to get the person talking.

It's OK to ask a question you didn't prepare. If one answer gets you thinking, you can ask another question.

An "All by Myself" Poem

When I'm alone I'm not by myself.
I have my book and my kitty to keep me company.
Together we snuggle and escape into fantasy and fiction.
All by myself in my favorite chair.
I feel like I am in heaven.

Writing a Biographical Poem

This poem is all about describing yourself or someone you know beyond just looks or appearances. It's writing about the inside of a person.

Feel free to rearrange, add or subtract things from the poem to make it just right for you. This poem makes a great gift for a birthday or an anniversary!

Here's how to write this poem:

First name ___________________
Mother/Father/Daughter/Son/Brother of ___________________
Brings to the world his or her ___________________
Lover of ___________________
Who fears ___________________
And desperately wants to ___________________
Wouldn't be caught dead ___________________
In the dark of night fantasizes about ___________________
And needs ___________________
Whose epitaph would read ___________________
Last name ___________________

Writing an Acrostic Phrase Poem

This poem form is done with a phrase you know well. It can be part of a song, a familiar phrase, a song title, an advertising slogan or even something you've heard a family member or friend say over and over again.

All you have to do is choose the phrase you're going to use and arrange the words vertically on the paper, one word for each line. Then play with it, inserting more words between them so it makes sense for you!

Getting Started

Advertising slogans are great for this: Can you hear me now? Or maybe something you hear your mom say over and over like: Have you finished your homework yet? Pay attention to what you hear during your day and you'll have lots of ideas for this poem!

A Biographical Poem

Evan
Son of Lynn and Barbara, Daddy of Ilana, Judy's soulmate
Brings to the world his or her energetic passion
Lover of equality
Who fears loss
And desperately wants to do what's right
Wouldn't be caught dead eating an olive
In the dark of night fantasizes about a peaceful world
And needs the freedom to express his thoughts
Whose epitaph would read, "a good man"
Gould

An Acrostic Phase Poem

Can I stay with
You and snuggle by your side and
Hear the sound of your voice as you read
Me my favorite stories? It's been a long time
Now since you've done that, and I miss it.

Writing an Onomatopoeia Poem

This poem uses sound words or actions to set a scene or event. Think of the old Batman series: Bam! Kapow! Boing! Those are sound effect words, and they are examples of onomatopoeic words that can be used to make a poem lively and fun to read.

Here's how you do it:

1. Think of an event. It could be as simple as your morning routine or as grand as a birthday celebration.
2. List the parts of this event as if you were writing a schedule, and leave a blank line between each written part.
3. On each blank line, write a sound effect word for added drama! Bam! You're done.

Writing a
"You Make Me So Mad" Poem

Sometimes people we know and love make us so mad! It's true. It doesn't happen all the time but when it does, boy do we notice! Those are the types of experiences that make for good poetry because they are about real feelings.

Has someone made you mad lately? Well, then get ready to write.

Here's how you do it:

1. Start with the line: You make me so mad!
2. List all those things that make you oh so furious. Make sure to put in as much descriptive detail as possible.
3. End with a line that tells the reader that you won't stay mad.

An Onomatopoeia Poem

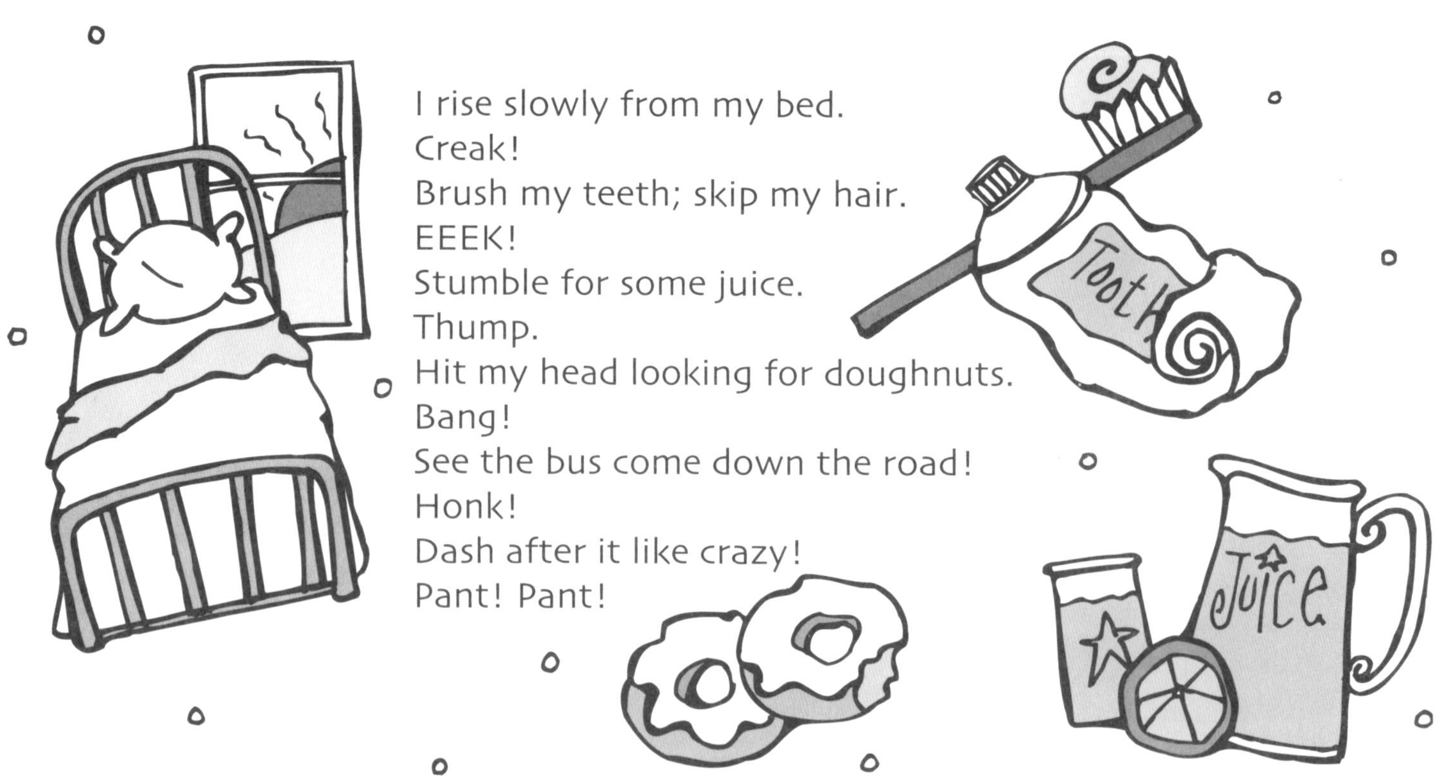

I rise slowly from my bed.
Creak!
Brush my teeth; skip my hair.
EEEK!
Stumble for some juice.
Thump.
Hit my head looking for doughnuts.
Bang!
See the bus come down the road!
Honk!
Dash after it like crazy!
Pant! Pant!

A "You Make Me So Mad" Poem

You make me so mad!
You barge in my room and go through my stuff.
You pull my hair when I'm trying to eat dinner.
You chew on my arm when I'm reading my favorite book.
You've thrown up on Granny's quilt that was made just for me.
But you're only two, so I won't stay mad for long!

Writing an "Odd Squad" Poem

This poem uses an odd number of lines and odd numbers of words for each line and that's about all you have to remember. What you choose to write about is up to you—just remember it's only seven lines and you have to count your words!

Here's how it works:

Line 1: 1 word
Line 2: 3 words
Line 3: 5 words
Line 4: 7 words
Line 5: 5 words
Line 6: 3 words
Line 7: 1 word

Writing a "Happy Place" Poem

Everyone has a place that they've visited or read about that is their happy place—a spot that is wonderful, relaxing and perfect. Sometimes it's an exotic place like a tropical island, but also it can be a place that's cozy and familiar, like a treehouse or your grandmother's featherbed where she would read to you when you visited. Whatever your happy place is, this is a chance to go there in your writing and stay a little while.

Here's how you do it:

First, think of your happy place. Then:
1. Write three words to describe it.
2. Name the happy place.
3. Write three reasons you'd want to go there.
4. Write how you would feel on a visit to this place.

An "Odd Squad" Poem

Homework
Gives me a
Huge throbbing horrible pain in
My head and it will explode and
My brain will be scattered
All around the
Room.

A "Happy Place" Poem

Sunny, warm and sandy
Hawaiian Islands.
The volcanoes, the luau, the hula dancing—
A place to relax.

Musty, cluttered and interesting
Uncle Mattie's art studio
All the paintings, the splashes of color on everything, the smell of turpentine—
A place to create!

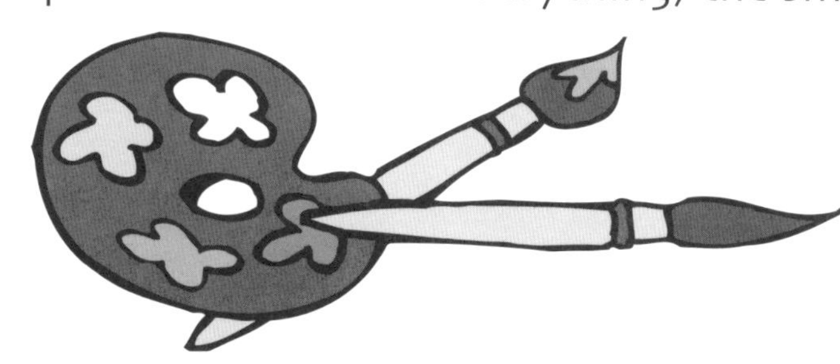

Writing a 5 Ws Poem

This is a great poem to help you describe hanging out with favorite family members or friends. To make this poem work, just answer the following questions about the things you do when you are just hanging out.

Here's how you do it:

1. **Who** do you like to spend time with?
2. **What** do you do together?
3. **Where** do you do it?
4. **When** do you have this time together?
5. **Why** is it special?

Writing a Recipe Poem

Have you ever read or followed a recipe? A recipe tells all the ingredients and steps you need to make something wonderful to eat. You'll be able to bite into your own delicious poem with this form.

Here it is:

1. Start with a boring day.
2. Then add a cup full of _____________________ (people).
3. Add a dash each of _____________________ (things you need).
4. _____________________ (things you do) and place all in
   _____________________ (where you go).
5. End up with a pretty cool day! (Or use your own ending)

A 5 Ws Poem

Bubbe and Great Grandpa
Cheating at Crazy Eights
While sitting at Bubbe's dining room table
Every time I visit—
I love how they let me win!

A Recipe Poem

Start with a boring day.
Then add a cup full of Deb, Bryce, Evan and Ilana.
Add a dash each of chips, dip, movies and craft supplies.
Munch, watch and talk and place all in Deb's living room.
End up with a pretty cool day!

Writing an Alliteration Poem

This poem uses alliteration, which is the repetition of a beginning sound in two or more words of a phrase (think of your favorite tongue twister!). This poetic effect can be used to create a unique image in writing.

Here's how you do it:

1. Think of something you want to write about.
2. Decide on a letter of the alphabet. For example, suppose you wanted to write about recess. You would need to choose a letter of the alphabet to go with that topic. Maybe you would choose S.
3. Think of a few words that are connected to recess that begin with the letter S. Maybe you would think of *screaming*, *swinging* and *scurrying*. Try to think of as many words beginning with the same sound as you can. Remember, these words MUST be connected to your topic or the line will not make sense.
4. Think of another letter of the alphabet and go through the same process.
5. Think of another letter of the alphabet and go through the same process.
6. End with this line: This is _________________ (topic you chose)!

Writing a "Looking Back" Poem

Here's a poem to help you look back at how much you've learned through the years. Just follow the form and repeat the pattern for as long as you need to in order to complete the poem.

Here's how you do it:

Line 1: It used to be hard
Line 2: *Name one thing you can do now.*
Line 3: *Name how you do it.*
Line 4: *Tell how you learned how to do it.*
Line 5: Now it is easy!

An Alliteration Poem

Swinging, everyone screaming, people scurrying for balls
Running right through rigid arms in football
Waiting for water while people take their time
This is recess!

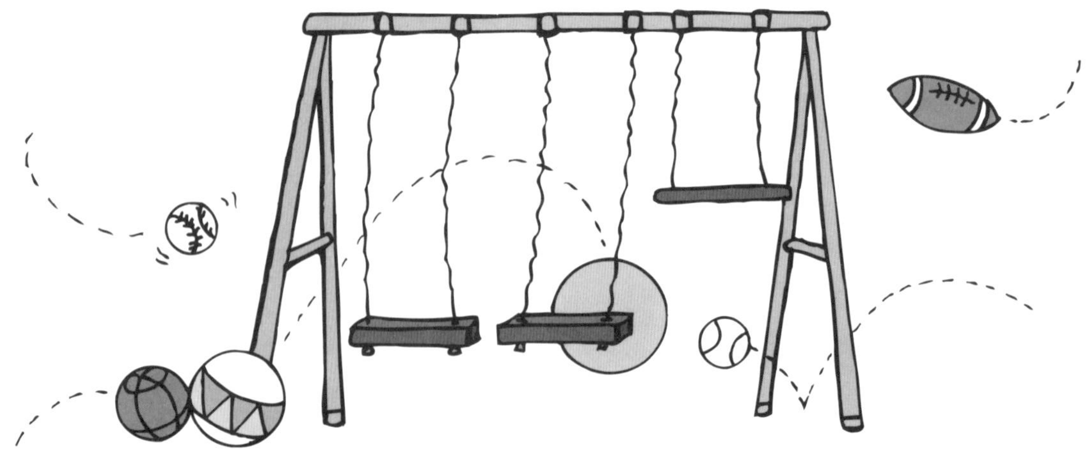

A "Looking Back" Poem

It used to be hard,
Writing in cursive
With my favorite ballpoint.
Hours of looping and copying and practicing—
Now it is easy!

Writing a "Friends Forever" Poem

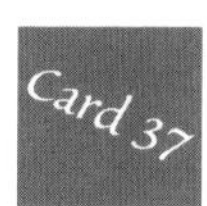

Friends make great topics for poetry. Sharing poems about the friends that mean the most to you is a wonderful way to express your friendship. Just follow this form to make the writing easy and fun!

Here's how you do it:

Line 1: Write the name of your friend.
Line 2: Write when and where you met.
Line 3: Write how your friend looked.
Line 4: Write what you used to do together.
Line 5: Write today's date.
Line 6: Write how your friend looks now.
Line 7: Write what you like doing now.
Line 8: Write how you feel about that friend.

Writing a Portrait Poem

Artists use charcoal, pencils or paint to create portraits. Writers use descriptive words and phrases to create portraits. Write a portrait poem about someone special.

Here's how you do it:

Line 1: Write the person's name.
Line 2: List three nouns associated with this person.
Line 3: List three verbs associated with this person.
Line 4: List three adjectives associated with this person.
Line 5: Compare this person to an animal.
Line 6: Compare this person to an element of weather or climate.
Line 7: Write a feelings statement about this person.

A "Friends Forever" Poem

Barbara
Moving in across the street, July 1998.
So cute in her pink dress with her long braided hair.
We went on the swings and splashed in the sprinkler.
August 2004
Tall and thin, with shoulder-length hair.
We talk on the phone and send instant messages.
I'm so sad that she moved away.

A Portrait Poem

Aunt Betty
Chickens, a butter churn, a shawl
Gardening, cooking, nagging
Soulful, kind, unique
Like a rooster so loud every morning
Like a hurricane that can roust you out of bed
She is country, but she is cool.

Writing a Favorites Poem

Everyone has their favorite things: things that are special to you, that you got from special people or special places. This is the time to think of them and write them down. Remember to be specific in your description so your poem pops in your reader's mind. A poem about favorites makes you grateful for all the wonderful experiences you've had!

Here's how to do it:

My favorite (place, thing, person) is ______________________.
My favorite (place, thing, person) is ______________________.
(Repeat as often as needed)
If only I could have a day full of favorites!

Writing an "I Wish" Poem

We make wishes all the time: when we blow out birthday candles, when we look at stars, when we throw pennies into a fountain. Here's a place to put your wishes down in a poem. You don't have to close your eyes or click your heels three times either. All you have to do is think about what your heart truly wants.

Here's how to do it:

I wish ______________________.
I wish ______________________.
I wish ______________________.
(Repeat as often as needed)
I wish, I wish, I wish all my wishes would come true!

A Favorites Poem

My favorite place is under the dining room table
Where it's cool and soft
And where my dog tells me all about his day.
My favorite thing to eat is anything with
Peanut butter,
Especially brownies.
My favorite person is anyone
Who doesn't treat me like a kid.
If only I could have a day full of favorites!

A "I Wish" Poem

I wish I was taller so no one could ignore me.
I wish I could put a steel beam across my door to keep my little brother out.
I wish homework was against the law.
I wish best friends would always stay that way.
I wish, I wish, I wish all my wishes would come true!

Writing a "That's Mine" Poem

Look around you. You have some stuff. Some of that stuff is just so-so, or things that you can live without. Then again, there are other things that are special to you for one reason or another. Paint a picture of these things with very specific words and phrases. Whatever those things are, this is a poem to celebrate all those things that are yours.

Here's how to do it:

See over there?
That (or those) _____________________?
That (or those) is (or are) mine.
That (or those) _____________________?
That (or those) is (or are) mine.
(Repeat as needed)
I have _____________________, _____________________ and
_____________________.
They're all mine and they tell my story.

Writing an "Oh No" Poem

We all have times when we are scared, nervous or uncomfortable. These things are just part of life, and one way we can get used to feeling these feelings is to write about them. Writing about them helps us understand these feelings a little better. This poem helps explore some emotions that will help us grow and mature.

Here's how to do it:

_____________________ frightens me.
_____________________ makes me nervous.
_____________________ scares me.
_____________________ makes my stomach hurt.
_____________________ makes me uncomfortable.
(Repeat as needed)
I'm going to take a breath until it all feels better.

A "That's Mine" Poem

See over there?
That neon orange sweater with a hole in the right sleeve?
That's mine.
That five-inch scar on my leg from my first bike accident?
That's mine.
That worn blue blankie my granny made me when I was born?
That's mine.
I have a teddy bear missing one eye,
a six-foot plastic pencil my dad won for me at the fair
and dried flowers from my best friend's birthday bouquet.
They're all mine and they tell my story.

An "Oh No" Poem

Thunderstorms at night when I'm the only one in the house frighten me.
Talking in front of the class makes me nervous.
When my mom gets a bad cold and stays in bed all day, that scares me.
Being caught in a lie makes my stomach hurt.
Seeing people argue and fight makes me uncomfortable.
I'm going to take a breath until it all feels better.

Writing to Yourself

This is a special kind of writing, very personal, just for you. Writing to yourself in a particular time and place is a way to freeze a moment in time. Write yourself at the beginning of a school year. Write every question you have about the coming year. *Who will be my best friend? What will my grades be like? Are the teachers going to be mean or nice?* Write them all down and then make predictions. Put the letter in a safe place and then let time go by. Open it on the last day of school. What's changed? How have you grown? All your questions will be answered and you'll have a personal piece of your own history.

Writing Tips

- This is writing just for you, so you can do it however you want!

Writing in a Journal

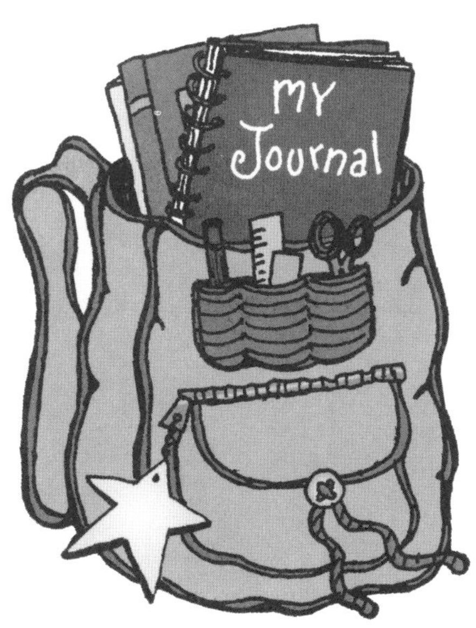

Journaling is good for the body and the mind. Getting your feelings out in writing can help you calm down, clear your thoughts, make up your mind, remember something happy, mourn something sad or try out a new idea. All of these things—and more—are perfect for writing in a journal. Your journal is just for you, so the next time you need a few minutes to pick yourself up, pull your thoughts together or plan your future—pick up your journal!

Here is a sample letter.

Dear Me,

  This is the day before my first day of fourth grade. I sure hope my teacher, Mrs. Thomas, is nice. She's a new teacher so no one knows what's she's like. Will she let us have extra recess? Will she sit us in alphabetical order or let us sit with our friends? Who's going to be my best friend? Will it still be Robin? I hope so because we've been best friends since second grade. I am 4 foot and 8 inches—how much will I grow this year? Will I be popular? Will my classmates like me? Will I finally understand long division this year? Will my handwriting get better?

  What things will change and which ones will stay the same? My favorite food is a buffalo burger—will that change? My favorite group is Black Eyed Peas. Will it be different by summer? All these things are on my mind now. At the end of the year, they will be answered.

Not sure how to start or what to write? Try one of these!

Write to rant: When you're angry or upset, writing about it can help you clear your head and get rid of your anger.

Write to celebrate: Happy times are always worth remembering.

Write to dream: Do you know exactly what you want your first apartment to look like? Or how you'd win the big game? Or what you'll say when you win an Oscar? Write it down, and someday your dreams may come true!